ENOUGH LIKE BONE TO BUILD ON

ENOUGH LIKE BONE TO BUILD ON

Poems by

Catherine DeNunzio

Antrim House
Bloomfield, Connecticut

Library of Congress Control Number: 2022912450

ISBN: 979-8-9855621-6-3

First Edition, 2022

Printed & bound by Ingram Content Group

Book design by Rennie McQuilkin

Front cover photograph by the author

Author photograph by Louis Gabordi

Antrim House
860.519.1804
AntrimHouseBooks@gmail.com
www.AntrimHouseBooks.com
400 Seabury Dr., #5196, Bloomfield, CT 06002

For Louis
and
for Luke & John

ACKNOWLEDGMENTS

Grateful acknowledgment to the editors of the following publications in which these poems first appeared, at times in earlier versions:

The Breath of Parted Lips: Voices from the Robert Frost Place, Volume II: "The Doily"

Connecticut Poetry Society website: "Irises"

Connecticut River Review: "Luna Moth" (as "Somewhere, Luna Moth")

Italian Americana: "First Fall Warblers," "The Snakeskin," "The Recovery"

Marin Poetry Center Anthology: "The Task"

Passager: "The Sovereign" (as "As You Are")

Scapegoat Review: "Holding On to Him," "What Matters"

Waking Up to the Earth: Connecticut Poets in a Time of Global Climate Crisis: "How to Feed a Child"

"Irises" was awarded an Honorable Mention for the Connecticut Poetry Society's Nutmeg Prize.

I am grateful to many, many people. Among them:

Laurie Cooper, Donna Nicolino, and Joan Seliger Sidney, whose insightfulness, honesty, and encouragement all those years ago are part of me. And for bringing us together, Gray Jacobik, who first lit the way. I carry the gifts of her exceptional teaching, and I remain humbled by her kindness and encouragement.

Rennie McQuilkin, whose generous spirit and brilliant mind continue to nourish and raise others up, and whose belief in my work made this book possible.

Especially and deeply, Sue Ellen Thompson, on whose writing doorstep I showed up as a stranger long ago. She welcomed me in, and with incisive intellect, inexplicable generosity, and indispensable guidance, she has fed and believed in me since. I could not have a finer mentor.

My dear parents and brothers, who kept me just close enough when my boat was small, and whose decency has always anchored me.

Luke and John: Language fails me. Beautiful, loved.

Most of all, Louis: I wake up on the grassy edge of dawn to you. I love you and love you.

TABLE OF CONTENTS

I. REACTING TO THEIR PRESENCE

II. ENOUGH LIKE BONE TO BUILD ON

"...the soul exists and is built entirely out of attentiveness."
– Mary Oliver

ENOUGH LIKE BONE TO BUILD ON

I. REACTING TO THEIR PRESENCE

First Fall Warblers

She sees them arrive as a flock, descend on the dogwood.
  They dip and bob like a mobile (blues and grays,
    bold yellows, black bars, white streaks)

as they devour the glossy berries.
  As she watches, a childhood memory returns:
    On a pine stump in a bed of moss—

her classmates' whispers left behind—
  she sat unafraid.
    The moss, deep green

and soft against her palms,
  became a forest of tiny trees
    reaching for light.

She smelled the damp vigor of decay,
  heard birds calling, leaves grazing leaves,
    and—muffled overhead—a distant airplane.

She noticed that, in a ray of light,
  her hair was strand after strand after strand,
    watched her own chest rising, falling.

The margins of her life dissolved.
  Now, the warblers lift and leave the dogwood stripped
    of berries. She steps outside, draws in the stillness.

Luna Moth

This morning as I roll down my driveway,
my mind busy with lesson plans,

I spot you, angled against the black lamppost.
I rarely see your kind: four wings

the green of promise, edged
in pink, tender as hope.

Beneath you, clematis climbs,
its papery purple buds still tightly closed.

If this is the first of your seven days,
the buds will have opened like hands

by the time you pass to darkness.
If the last, I am witness to your clinging.

Somewhere, although the world
ceases as I watch you,

a pair of siblings is called into a kitchen
for a wishbone contest only one of them will win.

Near a field of poppies being harvested for opium,
an egg case hangs like a thumb of glazed pastry.

Amid fragrant hay inside a fairgrounds barn,
a child sleeps, head against her dairy cow.

And in a canyon, a rattlesnake—patient,
coiled, motionless—waits for vibration.

By the time I reach the highway,
I understand my longing:

to feel your vast green around me—
and its futility, pink and raised as a scar.

Enough

They met as counselors at YMCA camp.
At times they swam laps at the Y back in town.
But the lessons they gave, the free swims

they guarded, were at the camp pond,
its waters verdant, redolent of life.
Seven years after telling her

she had not been enough for him,
he sent a card that said,
I will always have a place for you.

Too late. But still she dreams of him:
He pulls her toward him the way he did
those nights they met beneath the docks,

hinges shifting, groaning above them,
water lapping at their necks,
scarlet suits clinging,

while at the campsites,
the children slept
in quilted Coleman bags.

After, he turns
at the trail fork
as if she were not there,

just as he did the night
when all at once, came
an ambuscade of shrieks—

and then, the desperate cries of baby skunks
calling one after the other, the air still,
alive with their slain mother's scent.

The Snakeskin

Raised like a scar, my grandfather's name girdles
the century-old milk bottle I am holding.
Inside, a snakeskin.

In its day, the bottle held milk from his cows.
Late summers, the family men moved
bales from field to wagon to hayloft.

With relentless drive, and strength born
of strength used, my uncle tossed the bales
as a child might toss blocks into a storage box.

As a boy, his vocal and motor tics
meant he could not concentrate in school.
Some afternoons, he would be sent home.

But in the field and barn,
with the work horses and the cows,
all that neural firing was channeled.

Is it true the snakeskin came
from the barn and that he found it
on a rafter in the loft? True,

partly true—stories get passed on.
Maybe just their bones matter anyway.
And the directions encoded in the genes.

So we tell the stories
that bring my uncle back to us.
So my sons tic, too.

Harder these days for such boys
coiled with itch and energy,
with no set way to wriggle out of their skins.

Color

Out my kitchen window,
a veneer of rust, a landscape
of decaying leaves. In the oaks above,

burnt sienna clusters shiver
like tiny crumpled kites.
But pushing through the hillside:

myrtle, pachysandra, euonymus,
new spikes of Adam's needle. At the feeder,
pairs of bluebirds, goldfinches, scarlet tanagers.

For years, I found hope
in spring's green growth,
in the advent of breeding pairs.

Now such hope seems quaint in its allure,
cruel in the pleasure it nurtures.
Each Christmas Eve, when I was small

and tucked into my bed, I listened
hard for reindeer bells.
The next morning, my faith

was rewarded: Presents
appeared beneath our fairy-tale tree.
How could I have known belief would end?

Before the rending of my country—
the embrace of power, lies,
bigotry, revisions to our history—

I might have seen
meaning in all this growth,
all these nesting pairs.

Now, of what may I be sure?
Color.
Color for color alone.

Irises

*In dealing with color relativity or color illusion, it is
practical to distinguish factual facts from actual facts.*
– Josef Albers

This close-up photograph of a dog's eye
sends me to the old supplies:
paper, paste, pen, ink, knife.

I will cut her iris of yellow-orange,
stay factually factual in my choice of hues.
I mean to discover, not express.

For the swirling fur atop her orbit,
I will tear paper crescents of the blackest hue,
set them aside to stack around the iris later.

For her pupil, a patch of black less saturated,
like water shaded by woods. Then (see it seep
across the iris edge?) I will pull thin rivulets

of ink, let them bleed into the orange.
For the hazy reflection as she gazes,
an arc of silver foil from a chocolate bar.

I want you to know
the actual fact of your dog's eye
or of your lover's,

so that, however briefly,
you feel what you see.
As for me, I will savor

the dark chocolate from the foil.
But before I do—before I
cut & tear & paste & draw,

I will set a clutch of just-cut
irises into a vase,
the air surrounding them

reacting to their presence,
their presence to the air.
Nothing is itself alone.

Holding On to Him

He is shaving in the mirror by the open window
when the sun catches a strand of hair upon his chest,
glinting silver among the rest.

She murmurs. He turns.
She finds the strand, follows it,
grazing his skin with her fingertip.

She asks if there are more she has not noticed,
finds several woven through the rush of hair
across his groin. Within her,

something tightens, throat to navel.
The light above the mirror hums.
From the shaded cliffs, their sons'

voices drift through the window screen;
but she is thinking of the day
when she will see him slowly scuff his way

into the den in moccasins;
reach for the crossword on the table;
bend, pat the dog, gently tug one velvety sable

ear, then the other; at the window, check
the outside temperature, turn, head for their bedroom;
reappear dressed the same as yesterday to resume

the chore he'd set aside last evening. Later, she watches
as he walks down the driveway for the mail.
He pauses—thinking of the orchard, she can tell.

She gazes until she can see him clearly again—
shoulders square, hair not yet white—
watches for signs, tosses in their bed all night.

Miscarriage

While my fetus was alive, I sensed
its presence even beyond
my tender breasts, persistent nausea.
I felt an edgeless sense of its existence.

In the days and weeks after my miscarriage,
I was certain my fetus had chosen to leave.

What had led me to such fallacy?
A desire for a child so deep
that, still raw with loss, I reasoned:
If it had wanted to be with me,
it would have stayed.

That is what its brothers did years later,
turning at first slowly, then so quickly into men,
with no sense there had ever been
another who came before them.

My mother tried to answer
the only questions I asked out loud:
But where did it go? Where is it now?
Well, she gently said, *I suppose*
it's one with the universe again.

That's what my father is, and soon
she will be, too.
But the thought I cannot bear
is that one or both of my living sons
will also leave, by choice or otherwise.

Baby Gift

On my baptismal day, my godparents
gave me a sterling silver cup, on which
my monogram and date of birth
are still decipherable.

Its dimpled bottom seems to suggest
its smithy eased body to base
the way a seamstress joins
a full skirt to a bodice.

Instead, it documents how,
clutching the cup
in my fat fist, I banged it
on my wooden high chair tray.

Now young parents want to receive
soothing sound machines
for sleep, or feeding bowls
with suction cups for bottoms.

After they and their children are gone,
what useful object made to last
will someone hold while thinking,
She once held what I am holding now?

II. ENOUGH LIKE BONE TO BUILD ON

Dresses from Her Early School Years: 1961-1969

Welcome to the Exhibit

The exhibit considers how memory
reflects and influences our construction
and interpretation of meaning.

Included are six recalled artifacts representing
an eight-year period in the life of the subject,
as well as pertinent excerpts from her journals.

Before leaving the exhibit, visitors are invited
to document, in words and illustration,
artifacts from their own youth. Materials provided.

Introduction

*In March, I dream
of dresses from my youth.*

         −Personal Journal, 1996

They began in stores filled
with bolts of fabrics, drawers of patterns,
racks of notions, bins of remnants.

Sometimes she got to say what she liked.
Sometimes she was bored
and wanted to go home. Anyway,

her mother knew which patterns were tasteful,
which fabrics were out of season,
which colors would become her daughter best.

Artifact I, 1961

Cotton school dress of purple plaid
with black and moss-green lines.
Mother-of-pearl buttons,

their surface reminding her
of *gasoline swirling in parking lot puddles.*
Optional side-tabbed vest of lilac poplin.

School picture documents lace collar option.
I liked when my mother picked the vest alone.
Collar no longer extant.

Artifact II, 1962

Christmas dress of white piqué.
Puff sleeves, jewel neck, red bias trim.
Appliqued green holly with red berries.

Waist sash with *bow big enough*
to press into my spine at Christmas Mass
if I sat back against the pew.

Shown here over crinoline half slip,
the dress suggests cloth sculpture.
It had its own space in my closet.

Artifact III, 1963

Pastel orange school dress of cotton print.
*Ladies, drawn in black, rode bicycles
around my arms, down my chest, across my lap.*

Peter Pan collar. Black grosgrain sash.
Elbow-length sleeves with ruffled self-trim.
Dark orange rickrack at wide bottom hem.

She and her mother called it the Bicycle Dress.
Sometimes she wonders about its fate.
Does a scrap of it remain?

Artifact IV, 1965

Turquoise school coat of wide-wale corduroy.
Jewel neck. Lucite lozenge buttons.
Bell sleeves. Wide top-stitched hem.

Oversized butterfly print lining, unusual
for its time. *When the other girls,
pointing, began to laugh at me,*

*I ran across the playground
into the woods, wanting
yet hating my mother.*

Artifact V, 1966

Red print jumper of pinwale corduroy.
Fitted bodice. Gathered waist.
Self-covered buttons down the front.

Everywhere, blue forget-me-nots,
white edelweiss, leaves as green
as emeralds. Soft. Everything soft!

Artifact VI, 1968

Sleeveless sheath dress of teal velveteen.
Stand-up collar. Princess seams
designed to follow nascent curves.

Below the mini-skirted hem:
white lace she had not wanted.
Note color interaction with Artifact V.

In my dream, the colors vibrate side-by-side
like stop-sign red against a late-May lawn,
like indigo blue silkscreened on scarlet.

In this period she sensed herself
emerging from a forest into bright light.
I did not care that it hurt my eyes.

Calendar Girl

for Lou

Like me, others might recognize
your intellect, incisive and relentless.
They, too, might sense your sweetness.
And they, like me, might be drawn
to your square shoulders and brown eyes.

But only I am witness
to your latest obsessions—your discovery, for example,
of fresh fruit rather than preserves
on your peanut butter toast,
followed by your treatise
on berries versus stone fruits
and your reveries on the taste of each
as compared with that of their jam counterparts.

And only I—freshly showered and
having dropped my wet towel into the washer,

only I—having grabbed a cold, ripe
watermelon from the fridge beside it
(the largest, roundest one we've had this season),

only I—upon entering the kitchen
naked, holding the specimen like a trophy,

only I get your applause,
followed by,
Well. There's a farm calendar photo.

How to Feed a Child

Set on linen before the hungry child:
a bleached sea star & a bifurcated rock.

The five-fingered shell
is something fragile she can care for.

Intriguing enough to kindle desire.
Enough like bone to build on.

Enough like bone to say,
This was once alive.

She will marvel at the rock,
its ivory left & ebony right,

and trace the russet vein between.
Push her thumbs into its hollows.

Curl her palm
around its knobby shoulder.

Use both hands to gauge
its heft, her strength.

Wonder what
tomorrow's feast will be.

Replacing the Kitchen Table

Polished furniture reflected light
in nearly every room of my childhood home.

My mother valued pieces meant to last,
protected them with coasters, pads & tablecloths.

In my own home, the finished table
my husband and I had saved for as newlyweds

held mugs of hot morning coffee,
children's brimming tea party cups,

bowls of steaming soups & stews,
vases of houseplant cuttings & flowers,

markers & crayons & paints & paste.
But always, underneath, a pad & tablecloth.

Now, I want freedom from protection's demands.
I sand and paint and wax its replacement,

a second-hand maple table with matching chairs and
an extra leaf for when our grown children come to visit.

My husband and I lift our once-prized table
by its corners and carry it outside.

But when I remove the pad, I see it:
a gauzy, four-inch water stain.

All those years of training boys
to wipe up spills, peel back

soggy tablecloths, lift the pad, check
for dampness. Now the painted table

stands beside the same west-facing windows,
for however many years we two have left.

Prayer in Late November

She is partway through The Lord's Prayer before she realizes:
Since *who art in heaven* or so, she has been studying the titmice
at the window feeder. She recognizes she is of two minds:

the one connecting her act of watching to distraction,
and the one connecting it to God. She continues
the prayer, but what matters is her focus on the birds.

She notices what makes them titmice. Tufted crests.
Strangely large black eyes. Auburn-flanked gray bodies.
Hard work. Efficiency. Resolve.

Soon the ground will freeze. So, bed made, dishes washed,
laundry done, she retrieves her garden tools and heads outside.
She clips brush, drags the debris into a shelter for the birds.

Pushes a rotting log over the hillside. Transplants a beautyberry.
Cuts boughs of evergreens for her Christmas planters. Pauses.
Looks for other prayers to finish while she still has light.

The Task

Carrying in her beak
a twig three times her width,
a Carolina wren lands

on the narrow perch
of the birdhouse she has claimed
in the dogwood tree.

Again and again,
she seems to be trying to push the twig
through the birdhouse entrance.

How can it not have snapped,
I wonder, just before I realize
she's acting on a plan.

Bracing the twig in her beak
against the house, she slides it—
left, left, left—

until, with a sudden
sweep of russet head
above tucked wings,

she snugs the twig
lengthwise against her body
and disappears into the house.

Some days—
the task too huge, the opening too small—
I feel myself as driven

as any nesting wren.
I make the twigs fit
however I can, because these

are my wings, my beak.
With these and my resolve,
I build the life I can.

The Recovery

Since my husband's heart attack, I've learned to split wood
for the outdoor fire pit we sit by early evenings
after soup and therapeutic walks.

My son, whom I raised on *he or she,*
had shrugged his shoulders. *You can
do it, Mom. C'mon. I'll show you how.*

What I'd hoped to instill in him is there.
But does he carry, too, the errors
a first-time parent makes?

I worry that he must.
My husband thinks I'm too hard on myself.
Look at him. He's happy.

Sometimes at 3 a.m. when I
can't sleep, my errors trouble me.
But I can't know the answer to *what if,*

and I am tired of those nights.
So I build and light a fire
before night falls,

sit before it with my healing husband,
and pray my failures into smoke
that dissipates and falls to ash,

while the wood I split,
with my son's encouragement, fuels
a bonfire tenacious, purposeful, contained.

The Sovereign

Is this blossom of Queen Anne's lace
past her prime?

Around her,
like delicate parasols,

others at their most enticing
bob evasively at passersby.

But days ago, she sent
her umbels curling forward

into a seedhead, in which
she prepared her progeny.

Undulating and coiling, they
form a cavern fit for echoing,

I was young. I, too, enticed.
But she is done inviting.

Now her posture says,
Admire me or don't.

The Cake

Serve it under your magnolia
to your sons,
to your daughter-in-law,
to your small grandson
and to your husband
just home from the hospital.

Think of your mother
wrapped now in papery skin
who called you to the window
when you were small
to see birds and foxes
and took you to the high meadow
behind your house
and showed you corn cobs
the farmer left for deer.

The cake is good,
the blossoms magnificent.
You pass on what and while you can.

A Different Kind of Logic

Your children are not your children.
They are the sons and daughters of Life's longing for itself.
–Kahlil Gibran

Again my father says he wants to go home.
Again my mother tells him that they sold
their home years ago; this is home now.

Again and again, he asks her when they
will go to bed, where they will sleep, what is next.
Last night, he referred to my brothers and me

as adopted, though we were not.
And after seventy years together, he has begun
to forget that he is married to my mother.

She hands my father the phone in hopes my voice
will soothe his spirits as it always has.
He listens quietly as I tell him about my day.

But when I tell him that his great-grandson
spent all morning climbing, singing,
and digging for dinosaur bones,

my father cries out joyfully and declares,
Do you know why he does these things?
Because he has an eternal spirit of happiness.

I recount the exchange to my exhausted mother.
A moment passes. Haltingly, she speaks:
He could always see . . . he could always recognize . . .

the spirit within a person . . . and he could see how
that connected . . . to something . . . beyond what we can see.
I take the chance she has offered. *I wonder, Mom,*

if he means something other than the old house
when he speaks of going home. And last night,
when he called the boys and me adopted,

maybe he meant it in the way Gibran suggests.
In the stillness, before her duty-love takes over,
my mother is unburdened by a different kind of logic.

The Doily

The end-of-the-worlders say anytime now.
They blame the upsurge in deadly earthquakes,
hellish wildfires, catastrophic flooding
on those whom they condemn. They point
to Old Testament passages as evidence.

But tomorrow we will rise again at five,
slip into the dark outside, look
to the silver stars, and walk as
we have done for weeks.
An owl will call, *Who cooks for you?*
and be answered with the same.
In a patch of light from the neighbor's driveway lantern,
shadows of our dog's quick legs
will move again like bickering sticks—
Me first! No, me! No, me! No, me!
then vanish in the road's old dark.
Close to home again, Betsy's rooster
will crow his brassy boast

while on the bird's-eye maple table
that once belonged to Great-Unc on the farm,
a small fringed doily made
by someone long ago remains,
and on its tatted center square,
a tiny vase of eight gold mums
whose stems I beveled late
last night to keep them
until I-don't-know-when.

What Matters

I cannot visualize your heart as it appears in the film
of the intervention that saved your life.

I cannot picture the still-dying cells sloughing off,
or the inflammation that will not calm for weeks;

but I can see my hand circling
your warm chest, soothing and cooling

the still-hot embers of your damaged ventricle,
my intent running like a current

over your still-beating muscle—
new cells, new cells, new cells—

as your heart pumps its love-rich blood,
as your strong body, your stubborn will,

your joyful self rebuild what was
so starved for oxygen two Saturdays ago.

Last Paddle at Griswold Point

In the distance, a tepee-like structure,
its deadwood limbs bracing one another.
My brothers and I shore the kayaks
but keep our life vests on. Before long
the winds will gather, and we will have
to paddle hard to make it past the Sound.

John gets there first and calls us in.
It's a maypole with driftwood streamers.
The skeleton of a giant parasol.
An idea of shelter, as real as the bed-sheet tents
we built when we were children.
Although decades have passed since then,
it seems to us unfettered play incarnate, trimmed
with finds: a ping-pong ball, impaled; the bleached skull
of a laughing gull; a swimmer's goggles; the shell
of a horseshoe crab aimed towards the water; a blue whelk
wedged at the peak like a Christmas tree topper.

Now, before the waves begin their capping in the distance,
we hurry to add what has caught our fancy.
John, with his sculptor's eye, has picked
a hinged crab claw, proof that form follows function.
Charles hangs a miniature yellow airplane,
its pilot dreaming of adventure.
I nudge into a chink an intricate seedpod,
a reminder that I can always find intrigue in Nature.

Days later, rinsing dishes
at the kitchen sink, I picture the scene.

Before long, the winds
will turn as dangerous as the waters.
Who knows what we will find
if we return a year from now?

But waiting outside my house
this late September day: undiscovered treasures
my grandchild will bring to me,
before snow lays itself across all we see,
between us and whatever lies ahead.

ABOUT THE AUTHOR

Catherine DeNunzio received her B.A. and M.A. from the University of Connecticut. She has twice participated in the Frost Place Poetry Seminar. Before her retirement, Catherine taught middle and high school English for twenty-two years in several Connecticut public schools. In addition, she worked as a teacher consultant, freelance writer, public school partnership program coordinator, and private tutor. Catherine's poems have appeared in numerous poetry journals and anthologies. She lives in Ledyard, Connecticut, with her husband, Louis Gabordi. Catherine can be reached at cathdenunzio@comcast.net.

This book is set in Garamond Premier Pro, which had its genesis in 1988 when type-designer Robert Slimbach visited the Plantin-Moretus Museum in Antwerp, Belgium, to study its collection of Claude Garamond's metal punches and typefaces. During the 1500's Garamond – a Parisian punch-cutter – produced a refined array of book types that combined an unprecedented degree of balance and elegance, for centuries standing as the pinnacle of beauty and practicality in type-founding. They were based on the handwriting of Angelo Verge-cio, court librarian of the French king, Francis I. Slimbach has created a new interpretation based on Garamond's designs and on compatible italics cut by Robert Granjon, Garamond's contemporary.

Copies of this book can be ordered
from all bookstores including Amazon
or directly from the author:
Catherine DeNunzio
4 Chatham Berwick
Ledyard, CT 06339-2007.
Send $15 per book
plus $4 shipping
by check payable
to Catherine DeNunzio.

•

For more information on the work of Catherine DeNunzio,
visit www.antrimhousebooks.com/authors.html.
The author can be contacted at
cathdenunzio@comcast.net.